REFLECTIONS

Poetry by

ASHOK MANDAL

ZORBA BOOKS

Published by Zorba Books, May 2023
Website: www.zorbabooks.com
Email: info@zorbabooks.com
Author Name : ASHOK MANDAL
Editor : ASHOK MANDAL
Copyright ©: ASHOK MANDAL
Illustrations Copyright ©: PRADEEP AERI
Design, Layout: PRADEEP AERI

Title: REFLECTIONS

Printbook ISBN: 978-93-95217-68-2
Ebook ISBN: 978-93-95217-67-5

Zorba Books Pvt. Ltd. (opc)
Sushant Arcade,
Next to Courtyard Marriot,
SushantLok 1, Gurgaon – 122009, India

Printed by Thomson Press (India) Ltd.
B-315, Okhla Industrial Area, Phase 1, New Delhi- 110020

FOREWORD

When the mind speaks to the heart and the senses ,
stories emerge - some sad , some nostalgic , some
wayward and some soaring with intense emotions full
of thought and feeling .

When coloured with pain or joy, these stories take on a
new aura and meaning and are named Poems .
Many of these poems are random reflections that
acquired fame for their mirror of inner grief or longing
- such as Keat's " Ode to a Nightingale " or Grey's
" Elegy in a Country Churchyard " .

Ashok Mandal's poems are his personal experiments
in this genre where he delves in subjects that have
charmed him - such as MEMORIES , WISH , FRIENDS
et al . Like swirling images , the lines leave the reader
enchanted with the hearty and indeed the pathos of his
writing and wish the journey wouldn't end !

Thank you , Ashok , for this offering .

YOGESH CHANDRA , IAS

Mr. Yogesh Chandra is an IAS Officer who held several senior
posts like Secretary - Tourism , Secretary - Civil Aviation with the
Government Of India . He retired in 2000 with the rank of Cabinet
Secretary .

Mr . Chandra went on to become Secretary General of the
WTTC (World Travel and Tourism Council , India) .
He then helped to set up the Coca Cola India Foundation and was
it's CEO for 10 years . He retired in 2017 to write his first book ,
" The End Of Time ", which was published by Westland in 2021.

*When one walks under the Sun ,
Moon or just the Stars, one's shadow follows one !*

*My journey through life has been traced up
by my shadow even when I failed to walk .*

*During this trip of a lifetime , so many people ,
seas , rivers , flowers , birds , mountains ,
teardrops have come along !*

*Family , friends , lives , deaths , successes ,
joys – all in a package called life .*

*And in this walk of life ,
the tallest and most significant shadow of mine
has been my partner - my wife Shakun and
my exalted shadows - my children Kritika and Arpan
while seeking blessings from
my mother (Ma) and my departed father (Baba)
to whom I dedicate " Reflections " most lovingly .*

CONTENTS

Nature

Love

Life

Nature

AND QUIET FLOWS THE BASPA

And quiet flows the Baspa !
Descending from the
mighty Himalayas
throughout, the river kisses it's banks ;
many a times
wiping a few tears
and sharing the laughter
and sorrows of it's natives –
playing hide and seek
with the many rocks
coming on it's way –
full of antiques of
a truant child!

But now Baspa
the river, cries ;
it's murmur echoes
above the blasting of rocks
meant to reign in
through man - made dams,
all sins with accompanied garbage
dumped through it's throat –
almost choking the lifeline !

In a last - ditch attempt
the river tries to roar again –
looking for succour !

And suddenly,
quiet flows the Baspa again !

REFLECTIONS

THE DIFFERENCE

Bunch of blooming tuberoses
kept carefully on a china pot
in the decorated drawing room
blue sky can be seen
through the see - through window pane

a few dew drops !

There are enough flowers
and enough tuberoses
in the lawn outside
Difference ?
Honey bees are missing
from the tuberoses of the china pot !

SUNSET AT JUNGA

Looking from the
balcony of our suite
through the fading
january evening light
the decadent Shimla –
Once a Queen of the Hills !

Then the night fell !
through the bright sky
illuminated
by million stars
one paused to wonder
how the glories
can be ignited again !

Amidst the lurking
fear of a man - eating
Leopard who may be
on the prowl
while we inhale
the crisp air !

During our walk
along the dark pathway
we ponder !
can the hopes
be rekindled ?

Through the
deafening silence

of the cold night
then we embraced
a blissful slumber –
floating through dreams
those who dared
to touch the stars
lounging on
the edge of universe !

REFLECTIONS

In Pursuit of Salvation

In a frenzied river
my life is like a driftwood
that occasionally comes across
a few whirlpools only to be
rejected vehemently by them
and again continue to drift away

towards eternity...

The Deluge

River floods away trees , animals
and houses ,
even its banks ;
but when I will weep
my tears will flood away
The river itself !

THE CANVAS

The board
has been wiped clean
again,
of all the
memorial eye mucus –
a part of
unfailing morning rituals !

Images of
a desolated dead body
washed ashore,
hang outside !!

The reluctant waves
follow the current
with ephemeral
creation of
a few deltas
and
perennially delusive promises !!!

SPITI

You have waited !
Rising above the
abundantly flowing river
flanked by myriad
coloured and shaped mountains
You have waited !

The vast expanse
with immaculate barrenness
in solitude
from time immemorial
You have waited !

Amid simple village folks
solo traveller
sun, rain or snow
You have waited !

Amid reigns
of kings and demons
for thousand of years
amid despair and hopes
You have waited !

Today with the
chirping of birds
hide and seek play

of the clouds
alongwith sighting
of the proverbial rainbow
I declare
that
I have arrived !

KHAJJIAR

Finally we arrived
with our
winding dreams
in tow !

The constant stream
of the Paragliders
zooming by
in a flamboyant attempt
to touch and kiss
the snowcapped mountains !

" Lucky " the horse
is all set
for his and his master's
tryst with luck today !

The tall and dark
Deodar trees
overlooking the
green and vibrant meadows
soaked in dewdrops
from the last night's
offerings –
while keeping a watch
on the trickling
human faces
which will soon
turn into a storm

to be again swept away
to their monotonies
as the day ends !

While the cumulonimbus clouds
descend
on the unsuspecting valley ,
the old man
with his scarred face
bravely assures me
of the
eventual silver lining !

In the stillness
of time
amidst the
howling of wind
and despairs of
hungry hyennas ,
the white - robed
presiding ghost
just took his
midnight stroll !

While with her
lovable scars,
the full moon is
in her pristine glory ,
my dear,
that's Khajjiar for you –
Switzerland
delivered " Mini" !

THE HIMALAYAN BLUNDER

Thus
the plundering of the
mountains goes on
Misplaced sense
of development –
propagated by
the loudmouths !
Raging forest fires
driving dwindling
flora and fauna
to their
one - way annihilations !

Foraging by the locals
for a few drops
of water
while the snowfed
rivers originating
from the
mighty mountains ,
still somehow
strain to quench
the thirst of millions
down below !

The previously unseen
fury of the
unseasonal catastrophic
landslides ,

sweeping away
everything on way
including man - made
dam of pride !

High up from the mountains,
on a clear night
one may still
touch and feel
the Stars , Nebulas
and the Galaxies ,
while once the
abode of the Gods
and Mystics
now seriously looking
for relocation
to a compassionate world !

In the midst
of the fast disappearing
smile of
the truant boy
and nonchalantness
of the womenfolk ,
the remote village remains
tucked away
around now
not so confident peaks !

It appears
we ,
like the nomadic shepherd
with his ever - wandering flock
blissfully tracing away
the rugged mountains
from season to season ,
not knowing that
the ground below his feet
may slip away anytime –
destined being born
as the most
spectacular mountains
those rest on a
timebomb
called " Zone - Five " –
the severest earthquake prone zone !

While I gaze at
those two
sacrilegious saints
on a hunger strike
trying to safeguard
the well - being
of the Holy Ganges
while millions
attempting to wash away
their accumulated

sins and earthly worries ,
I wonder
whether
these sages are
aware of the
futile fate
which befell
on the Famous Professor
fighting the just causes ,
at the alter
of doom !

This , in a nutshell
my friend ,
is the ultimate disaster
in the brewing
called
The Himalayan Blunder !

MANALI

Once again
I am
in the midst
of her ever welcoming
aura !

Encompassed
by the
innumerable trees
laden with
red and green apples –
busy showcasing
the contrasts of
dazzling colours !

Mountain birds
in playful shrills
often displaying
eternal love
in abundance !

At a touching distance
from the balcony
of my room
the surrounding mountains
inviting me
to join them
in their play
of early morning shades ,

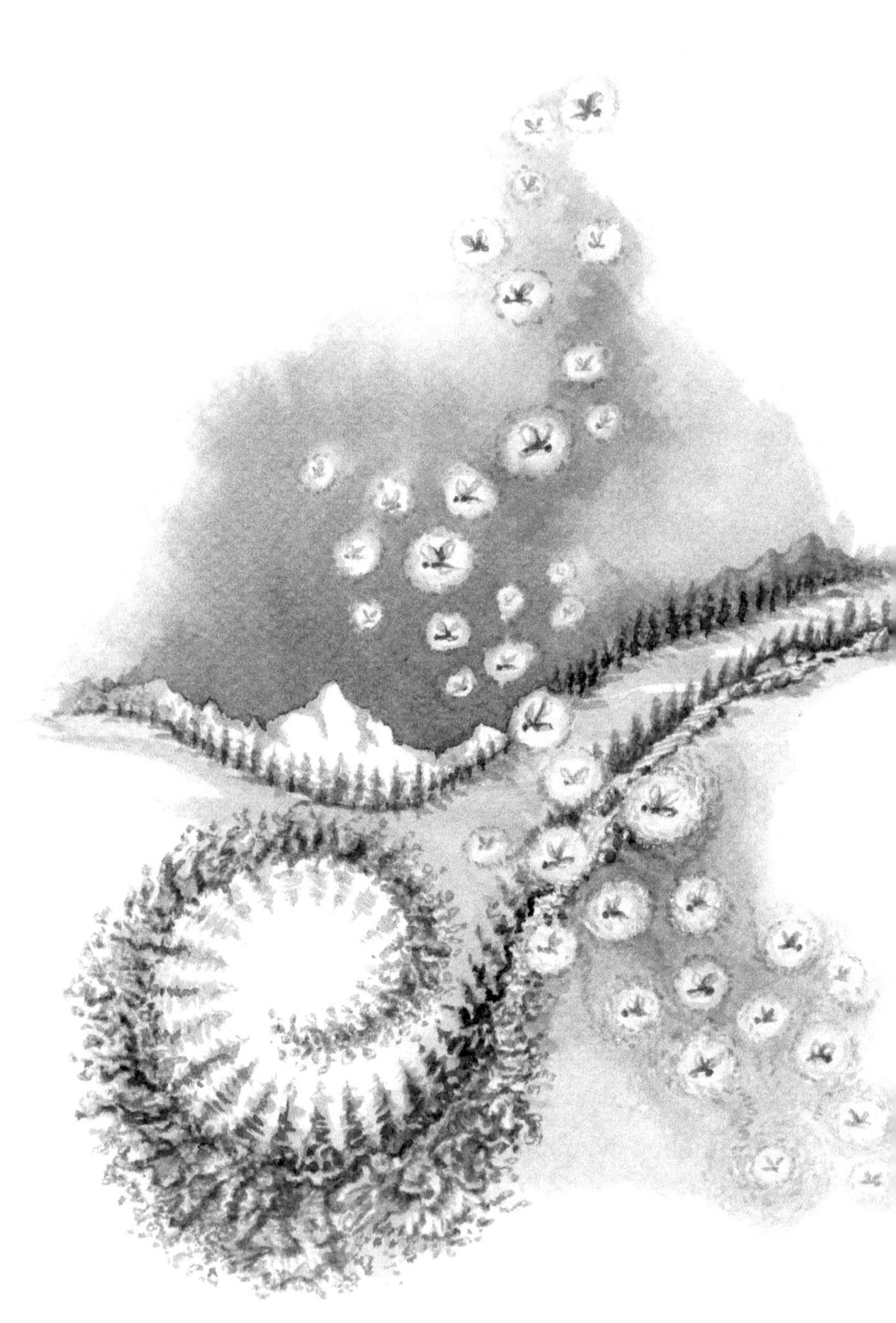

enabled by
the yet to be
visible Sun !

The gurgle of
the nearby stream
nudging me
to go out
and feel her
cool vibrancy !

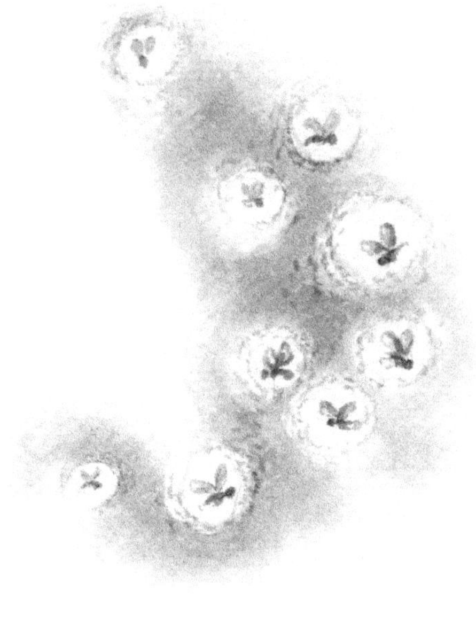

On the cobbled pathways
of the
still sleeping village ,
I am being greeted
by the
crisp and pure breeze
while the neighborhood
" Man's Best Friend " trying to extend
his unsolicited company !

The day passes
with the
extreme sense
of satisfying explorations ,
genuinely thanking
the Creator of such
divine beauty
while trying

to nudge aside
the visions of
criminal unending
savage exploitations !

As the evening falls
a clear sky
gets illuminated
by a plethora of
myriad Stars
and Milkyways ;
a couple of fireflies
trying hard
to showcase
their flickering lights
as if
in competition !

As I snuggle into
my cosy bed
for a good night's sleep ,
one more time
I wonder on
Manali
that epitome
of perpetual vivacity !!!

DREAMS

A life without dreams
is a life
devoid of any passion –
as waking up from
a seemingly good sleep
with a blank mind !

Dreams are like
a maze of colours
of a fantasy land
compelling our body , soul
and spirit to achieve the goals
which we chase
continuously !

Dreams are buffers
between hopes and despairs –
between living
and the dead !!

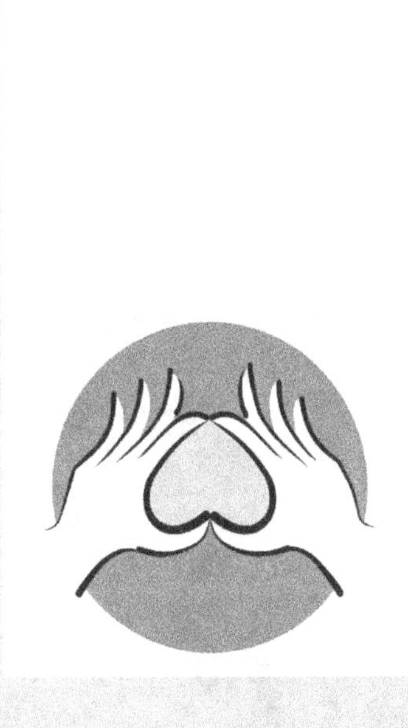

Love

PRAEFATIO

More lost than being lost
and more dead than being dead
merged into another name
which is unknown to me
will I ever be able
to know you
as before ?

While my winged dreams
galloped through milky ways ,
nonchalant with your pulsatingly perfect
phenomenal strength ,
alone I remain awake and awaited
for Morpheus
to struggle with conscious realities
and
perhaps ,
to receive a few bouquets , brick-bats
and a romantic cremation !

Love does not believe in pleonasm !

FATHER

FATHER is the entity
who lives even
after his shadow retreats !

An embodiment of inspiration
that lingers through
the lifetime !

An epitome of strength
which supports
as a rock !

The childhood
memories of togetherness
filled with little dreams
which help continuously
to mitigate the pain
of growing up !

Father, who reassures
the best ;
either being close to
or away from you –
as the ultimate saviour !

MOTHER

Mother
separated from the
umbilical chord at birth
till enjoined
at the last sigh !

Mother
always the close confidante
the assimilator
of all pains and sorrows !

Mother
The indomitable well - wisher
Shielder of all curses, dooms
and evils
the hawk - eyed sentinel !
The always-losing partner
of the hide and seek game –
played in the blossoming
years of the childhood –
the unfadable mother !

Mother
that epitome of patience
that colossus of strength –
the eternal mother !

FROM ME TO YOU

Why is that jasmines have bloomed and died
in laughter and silence
season to season ?
why is the way to crematorium endless ?
why can't I adorn your feet
with anklets of impatient whispers ?
why is that I always sought solace in examples ?
why has existence become an occupation enough ?
why has love become a word , best forgotten ? !

For me
the song is over !
over the delights of your flickering eyelids
that used to lift my eyes to yours !
Down the memory lane , at last
we gave a ceremonial burial
to our haunting promises !
while my eyes wait for the snow to melt
certain belief affirms me
that you would be defeated
by my tears !
in your absence
every morning and evening the sun plots my death !

I sighted the pandemonium of colours
in the rainbow
and
was declared a paranoid schizophrenic !

R.I.P 1983

Rains have come and gone
I never breathed so much
not so much as you
Rains have come and gone !

I do not understand when
you pretend to love or smile
I do not understand when
you shed your affluent tears !
Your apparent confusion
and imperfect images
convey a feeling that is perfectly definite !

I do not understand
when telephone rings of death bell
and no-nonsense agony envelopes
with cancerous memories !
I do not understand
when solitude comes blessed !

I learnt to live in my four - walled shell
protecting dreams from daylight
and your interpretations ;
Prehaps you speak of nothing
when I speak of love !

I do not understand
When I pity me ;

surge of meaninglessness
forms a face - drugged , ravaged and sad !

I did not realise
when fatigue had crept in
when adolescence aged
Old , pale and skeletal !

For the last time
I wish I could witness
The mythical dawn
with your once gleaming pupils
dark and still !

I feel my frozen nerves
and acrid tears
pale rose petals and silent faces
emotions abundant !

I hear a bored priest
delivering the sermon
' Suffer , you bastard ! '

OCCUPATIONAL THERAPY

From dawn to dusk
from hybernation to death
till reincarnation
I sketch you
with exiled memories
agonies and ecstasies aplenty !

From dawn to dusk
I toil
the locals , 153 , the airconditioned suffocation
and chromatic people
the run-over man or the flabby leper
or the scurvy-affected orphan
selling Saibabas !

Occasionally our entwined destinies
witness an ephemeral fire
and sets the night
with a languid trance
I inhale courier of cancer
and try to brave the metaphor of dying leaves –
moment of despair is ageless concourse !

From dawn to dusk
I recycle myself
for the spring may invade anytime !

THE REPRIEVE

For once
let me pluck the flowers
for you
let the crucified thoughts
resurrect
let me lift the painted veil
that is called life !

For once
let me dream again !

In the travail of existence
framed are the shattered memories
while heaven stands witness
of the nuptial of life and death –
let me rekindle our burning pyre ;
If only the world was another Noah's Ark !
Noetic you
I don't lament for the absence
of your eulogy !

For once
let me like the slush
the hazy drizzles ;
let me wade through
overflowing crowd , crammed cities
heaps of no - nonsense agonies
forlorn impatience , sisyphean myths
beyond bread and butter !

chanting of fire hymns by the ocean
keeps the universe
enthralled in an immaculate silence ;
while the snow melts at some
distant mountain
I , the lustral rose ,
try to transform
the annihilated self
into the spring sonata
in an all too familiar repertoire !

For once
Buy me some peace , some pain
some sleep
tenderly gift - wrapped
on my next reincarnation !

METAMORPHOSIS OF A PSYCHEDELIC

Hypnotized
as I am
spread my delirious look
to infinity
in search of a stimulant you
you
that had been an eternal silence !

Remembering
those anonymous ecstasies
and your fragile promises
often I lapse into cathartic slumber
amidst an anguished breeze !

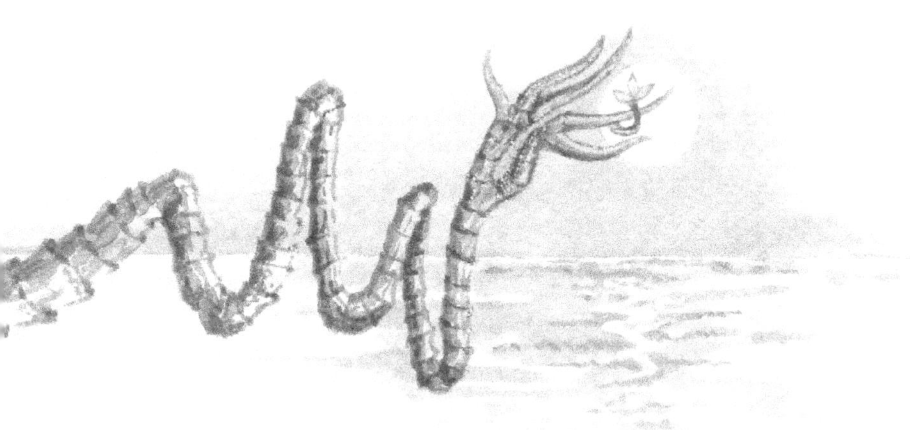

Suddenly
I hear a murmur –
personified facsimile of yours !

Emergence of a forgotten despair
from the rumbling of pebbles
of a shattered dreamhouse
resurrects me from the oblivion ...

EPILOGUE

With
asthmatic nights
a pauper heart
an empty pocket
a lung cancer and acute pain
and your request for a poem
I have not dreamt since long !

Through the smoke of cigarettes
you too , look smoky ;
burning all memories
alone I remain awake and await for Morpheus –
with a cremated heart ;
and I feel how happy is childhood !

To the songs of the sea
or to the Pole Star and the Moon
or to the Rose
I am too aged ;
today the churned sea is dark - blue
with it's poison
an ill - fated earth searches around for Mahadeva
her tears of agony in the frozen night !

Staring at the infinity
I only errupt dark rosettes of blood
and a feeling
that poetry is not possible anymore
grips me !

THE PHOENIX

Little gusts of wind
blew your frizzed hair
to the eternal sea
along with waves !

When I held your hand
you promised the earth to me
songs came to me
without any foretaste , without warning ;
in my flight of fancy
with copious clouds ,
you took me by my hands
and led me across the sea
to an awkward pause !

This day
when I ask for my sleep , my pain
your melancholic smile
gives a feeling
as if I knew nothing of love !

You scream
beware the electricity in my hair ;
but this is no suicide –
only a sudden electrocution
painlessly precise !
May be dreams are better left the way they are !

Suddenly the rain came
and I find you were gone
the great banyan tree branches
swept the ground
bushes glowed through the rain !

Amid blue fireflies
my foolish desire of destruction
vanishes ;
I listen to the
pouring of rain
crickets
and the anguished breeze
And grip my hands
around my breast .

I wish
I could drop my heartless love
my blue despair
my soliloquy
to see
if the icy water
still stirs !

Oh poetry !
If I could only believe
that this place would
ever see you again
I would set the walls a blaze
with passionate declarations !

SOMETIME SOMEDAY

While I shiver with your electrifying
hair and often bleed
in self-inflicted pain
you hum for me
in darkness !

You lock my palm with yours
and more often fail to keep pace with
the delirious raging wind
or the primeval hungry light
or the cluster of madness –
which is me !

You relent all these being temporal !
a sudden and grave silence munch
the winter wind
solitude hauls me ;
from the dark sea
a hypnotic tide brings ashore
that stale and perpetual message

Behold , the future sky may beckon
Sometime , someday !!

CAN YOU... ?

Come nearer
hold me with the warmth of your heart
darkness all over
rings of smoke
battering of bats , howls of dogs
nerves and veins are freezing away
can you save me ?

Dew drops on the grass
it is feared , they will dry up
as soon as it dawns ;
awakening songs for the world
atom bombs , rockets , missiles ,
uranium and cyclotrons
sources of new energy !

Dilapidated and faded houses
standing like skeletons of beheaded ghosts –
prehistorical creatures !

Lazy steps of the homebound drunkard
mad bells ringing away at the distant church
deep slumber like thick fog of a hill station
nerves and veins are freezing away
can you save me ??

MADRIGAL

Till today
I search you Shabari
from Atlantic to Pacific
I follow
the ganges
along her nocturnal travail
along her lapping waves !

In this humid night
heavy with animal scents
you only notice my pretension
of being lost –
but I don't realise
that I am losing
losing a game – that is life !

While I await cutting unbiblical chords
blood and seasons mingle
and time liquefies ;
your thoughts entwine my languid arabesques ;
tottering on the edge of equilibrium,
I hear a strange bird – cry
shrill yet melodious !

Everywhere except in my heart
life is suspended ;
Do you hear Shabari
someone is weeping
with affliction and wonder ?

But echo only returns
Shabari doesn't !

The Reign of Evil is Over

Curtains drawn
everyone is up
the hour of departure has struck
your ceremonial attire
manicured palms , jingle of bangles
fill the air
with a funereal solemnity
Love , even when filled with hate
doesn't have that sullen face !

All badness consummated today
everywhere , even hours away from here
Hyenas won't sniff
the nonexistent wind
I , the freelord of a strange kingdom
witness garlands of stars
hungdown from the black sky
and declare
The reign of evil is over !

Come my love,
The moment of celebration has begun !

OPUS – I

Oh you beautiful rains
the chilly drizzles
the copious clouds like a carpet of jasmines
the truant Sun in his majestic splendour
the paranoid rainbow
the tapestry of plethoric Gulmohur
the forlorn stars
the liquified time !

Do you know the reasons
for my stirred heart
the violence of my excitement
this symptom of love

with its quivering ardour –
it's impatience , it's bewilderment ?
this fragile patience
this passionate languor
this reverberating heartbeats
my solace
my rejuvenation

is my love , Shakun ?

OPUS – II

And then love arrived
from the distant galaxies
along milkyways
through fair of stars and their sparkling icicles
from the forgotten despairs
amongst confusion of my spirits
amid interrupting raindrops
amid crimpson glow
that precedes
dawn at the Kanchenjungha !

When the whole world looked
pale and skeletal
when my legs became weak
drunk with accumulated fatigue
when the wind gasped for breath
when darkness began to coagulate
when life seemed a contradiction
and idea of flight seemed winning !

Then she confided to me
and love really had arrived !

HAPPINESS

Happiness is the butterfly
that flits
from flower to flower
savouring the sweet taste
of honey ;
with plethora of colours
on its wings –
like a rainbow
over the dark clouds !

Happiness is
the state of mind
that always seeks
out of monotony of life –
momentary or everlasting !

DAUGHTER

Our first born
a bundle of joy
arriving after a
particularly trying
phase in life ;
innocence personified !

Never realised
when she grew up
from playing
hide and seek
to a formidable girl ;
indomitable , balanced and confident !

Barely occurred
when she set feet
on a fairy land
to chase her
academic dream
to be followed by
a dreamier career ,
while pursuing
her passion for
dancing with the stars !

As the days roll over
she ensures
through her unfailing love
demonstrating

that distance is just a number !

The seasons come and go –
the trees and the plants
pass through the cycle
of being green to being chauve !

Under the dim - lit
crescent moon ,
suddenly I see in her
a mother – reflected !

SON

Son
that package
of happiness
who grew up suddenly
engaging
relentless mockfights
and identifying every car
when children of his age
barely started walking !

Son
who does not
wish to be bound
by
conventional laws
even when sieved
through the preachings
of theoreticals !

Son
that voracious reader
and collective
of diverse emotions –
exalted embodiment
of
one's fascimiled reflection !

Son
who regales

while making
our hearts reverberate
through
his soulful music
and
made us
sail through
with his
melodious notes –
the hopelessness
of the pandemic !

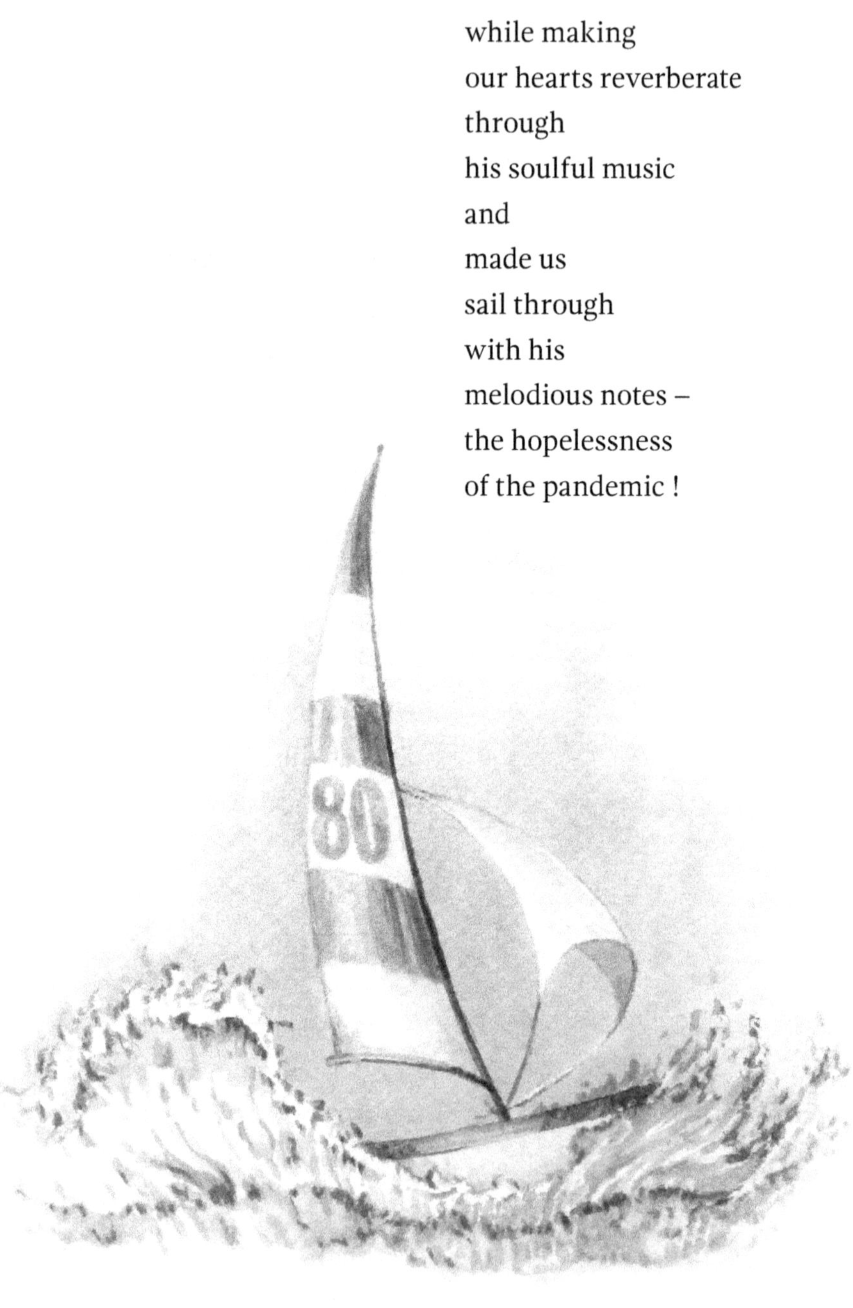

Son
a small child
who mightily clutched
onto you
with
a forlorn face
everytime
it dawned to him
of my next worktrip
away from home –
precursors
to the
eventual final separation !

Son
who wades through
a bunch
of solemnities
of life
but stands
as an infallible rock
for our
dissipating memories !!!

FRIENDS

Friends
are those
who
make you find
the lost child
in you
everytime
you are together
while the time
is forced
to pause !

Friends
are those
with whom
your so - called
guarded secrets
never stop
tumbling out !

Friends
are those
who agree
to disagree
for all matters
temporal !

Friends
are those
who make you
treasure
the minutest
pleasures
of life
while
the world
may be
glistening with
manicured pompousness !

Friends
are those
who held your hand
when
the earth
below your feet
seemed to be
sinking in !

Friends
are those
who made
the darkness of night
to face
the dazzles
of the daylight
over bottomless glasses

of
shared intoxications !

Friends –
that flock
of
diehard life jackets
those keep you afloat
in
the times of turbulence !!!

THE HOME COMING

Home coming
is
when
a part of your heart
gets lodged back
into
it's original place !

When the DEVI
visits
her earthly parents' home
with her children
in tow –
albeit for
a few days in a year !

When
the longing
for
a simple hug
merges with
the excitements
of WhatsApp calls –
with or without
occasions !

When muted pulpitations
of
the impending

departures
pave way
for the much - needed
stabilization !

Home coming
is
when that
myriad migratory bird
from the farout world ,
during it's
yearly sojourn ,
drops by
at our lawn
and
breaks that
stupendous news
of return
of the pearl
of our eyes !!!

Life

Fatal Attraction

I gaze through the window
The train is moving fast
I hope it does not meet
with an accident !

Darkest sky
and lots of stars
I want to shoot down the stars
with a gun
one by one
to this earth !

I wish to possess a gun !

In Anticipation of a Metempsychosis

Arising from a drugged sleep
I brush the memorial eye - mucus
and stare at the falling of NEEM leaves
through the window bars !

The winter is approaching !

Love of blue BANARASI sky's night
metamorphosed into widowed memoirs
of every misty dawn –
clotted with pains , defeats , wilderness ,
halts abruptly !

And
entering into my skeletal remains
crippled wind of an unknown ice - age
keeps on shaking off
bones
one by one ...

Post Mortem

Through the death of dreams
birth of that unborn baby
even stars and flowers shuddered !

Many a times I wondered
what difference does it make
of my being or not being ?

But
your thoughts
like high tides
swept away my hesitations ;
like a storm - stricken crow
I stood up at the midnight
frightened
and
amidst the light of that oblique moon
I walked away cautiously
leaving behind the memories...

LET IT BE

Suddenly I realise
salty water recedes
from the paradise
ignored pains are awake
in the dark
with the crowd of dead glowworms
and a scorched moon –
crippled and dying promises
have been lying in the dark blind lane
for ages !

Let them remain there
with the burnt moon
after sunset
and
in the crowd of dead glow worms .

IN ODD HOURS ...

Every time he was refused
was that any mistake ?
any sin ?

In this late hours
when the whole memory
is like a white washed wall
bloodless
when
all noise mix up
with the never ending sound of eternal rain
and
the darkness jumps down
with a peculiar anger !

Then
murmurs
speechless repentation
with bent knee
' forgive me , forgive me '
in that soundless , memoryless
hall !!

The Awakening

The awakening
that the
holy water
is wanting
in atoning
centuries of
accumulated tendentiousness !

That
we are chained
once again
in our
own prisons
of desperations !

That
the relationships
can be
as fragile
as your
possessed cutglasses !

That
for most leaders,
the leadership
is another word
for conceited !

That
prick of a jab

might be actually
propitiating
immortality !

That
it may be
the time
for the mankind
to relocate
to that elusive space
called Utopia !

That
the Gods
are in a
dilemma
while
granting salvation !

That
every exhalation
is a testimony
of you
being there !

I am even told
that Kanchenjunga –
the Sleeping Buddha,
may decide
to locomate
if the invocations
are just !

Apocalypse Now

And the Pandemic struck !
The Mighty Leaders from
their fabled glass houses

declared shut - down –
in a futile attempt to hoodwink
the Monster !

While people got caged
in their own dwellings ,
Orphaned Millions marched
the Highways and the Railroad Tracks
with families in tow ;
Thirsty , starved , sick and tired ,
towards their own mirage - like utopias !

While alcohol found another life - saving use ,
being masked and keeping distance
became the new normal !
The days became eerie
and the nights spectral ;
even the strays wondered
to remain quiet !

For once , the myriad birds
and the bees
dropped by the cities;
places which do not otherwise

host such guests anymore!
And the flights of fancies
got restricted to
the original winged fliers
while the humans
remained grounded !

REFLECTIONS

The Millions lost
on how to feed themselves
and their near and dear ones
while for the children,
the learnings became distant !

The Theatre of Life
circled around those
protective - geared fellow humans –
the health workers
while occasional sirens
of the ambulances reminded –
be ready to play your part !

With clanging of bells
the Leaders tried to invoke
the divine power
which somehow kept on
reminding
us becoming the
Children of Lesser God !

And while the search
by the proverbial Hippocrates
for that elusive
Asclepion potion continues ,
the yearning to feel
the warmth of once again
embracing the loved ones
keeps on leaping –
a la Phoenix !

DEATH OF A POET

Today
a search for the heaven's gate
across the sea of darkness
today
scores of dry amaranth
amidst draught and famine
in Indra's flower garden
today
in the cloudless sky
a condolence meeting
of a million stars !

Have they got the death news
of the poet ??

AND THE MOROS
RETURNS

Just when
the World started crawling
in an attempt to
stand up

Just when
the daily wager
managed
to get
an apology of
a meal
for the family

Just when
the weary healthworkers
paused
for a
deep breath

Just when
the caged children
started to feel
the smell
of their classrooms
again

Just when
the aged parents

were waiting
for those treasured hugs
from their loved ones –
attempting to make
their annual trips
from the distant lands

Just when
the freshly minted
graduates
palpably awaited
for their encounter
with
the real world

Just when
those struggling businesses
attempted
to crawl out
of their hibernations

Just when
the starry - eyed couple
waited
to tie the knot
of their
customised
roller coaster ride

Just when
I thought
I could

go out again
and circumnavigate
the world

Just when
the elusive Gods
started opening
their venerated doors
for the
ultimate human salvation

Then
almost
with a vengeance ,

the MOROS *

returns !

* *The Primordial Deity
in Greek Mythology and
the Personification of
Impending Doom !*

THE KNOCK OF APOPHIS

Another sun goes down
with that slips again
the hope
of resurrection !

Churning the cauldron
of pseudo - religious concoctions
and plethoric fake - believes ,
the thickheaded masters
thrive !

The ravenous mother
at the street corner
just sold her baby
while we lost
our collective soul !

In a dystopian world
while the edifices
of the dead
soared skybound
riding on the vanity
of the Powerful,
below , the millions
scampered for the crumbs
in pursuit of survival !

Even the nature decided
to play the dance

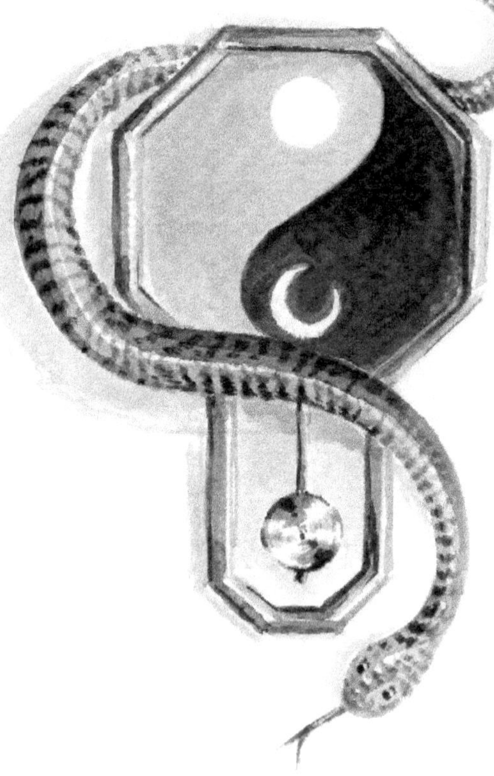

of annihilation
leaving behind
ravages of wildfires
typhoons , quakes and flashfloods –
snapshots of a
cataclysmic existence !

Another sun goes down
and the grip of
the dark night tightens ;
the rudderless youth
tries to pierce
his vision to the sky
through the ceiling
of his solitude!

Amid the inconsistent steps
of the vagabond drunkard
and howling of hungry dogs
the piercing wind
reminds us
that
the knock of Apophis *
may just
turn out real !

* The ancient Egyptian demon of chaos .

THUS SAID

They said
love must be
crucified
if it happens
between the faiths !

They said
history was
manipulated
and hence
must be rewritten !

They said
that round - rimmed
semi - clad Messiah
for many ,
was a fraud
and hence
must be hunted down
even if
he was dead !

They said
the detection
of the devil
through the
myopic clouds
was impossible
even when

armed with
that all pervading
scanner !

They said
Gods are
afraid of
falling
inauspicious shadows
on them
and hence needed
only
selective seekers !

They said
celebrate
the shots
against that
almost invisible
monster
while millions
fell wayside !

They said
they would
transform
the Holy Ganges
holier
so that

one can
wash away
one's misdeeds
and merge
into them !

They said
they are here
to liberate us
from all
those years of
inhuman bondage !

THE QUEST

While it is time again
to live that
life
in isolation !

While it is time again
for the abandoned parks
to host
the myriad birds !

While it is time again
to skip that
reassuring hug ,
lest that
invisible monster
sneaks in between !

While it is time again
for the emaciated
migrant
to scurry back
to his
dilapidated existence !

While it is time again
for the families
huddle
more in fear
than
in joy !

While it is time again
for the
deserted roads
leading to
the choked crematoriums !

While it is time again
for the people
in power
to rant about
what went right
and not
what is
going wrong !

While it is time again
for that
any moment knock
of the
round - fangled
Satan !

May be it is time
for
the weary world
perspicaciously
waiting for
the Blue - throated
Saviour –
once again
gulping down
the fallacies
of human boisterousness !

WISH

If only
my winged dreams
could gallop
from continent
to continent ;
from stars to stars
from galaxies to galaxies !

If only
I could erase
with my paint brush
the dividing lines
from
the World Map !

If only
I could
talk
to that
fleeting sparrow
now visiting
my lawn
on his
eventual extinction !

If only
I could
wipe away
forever ,

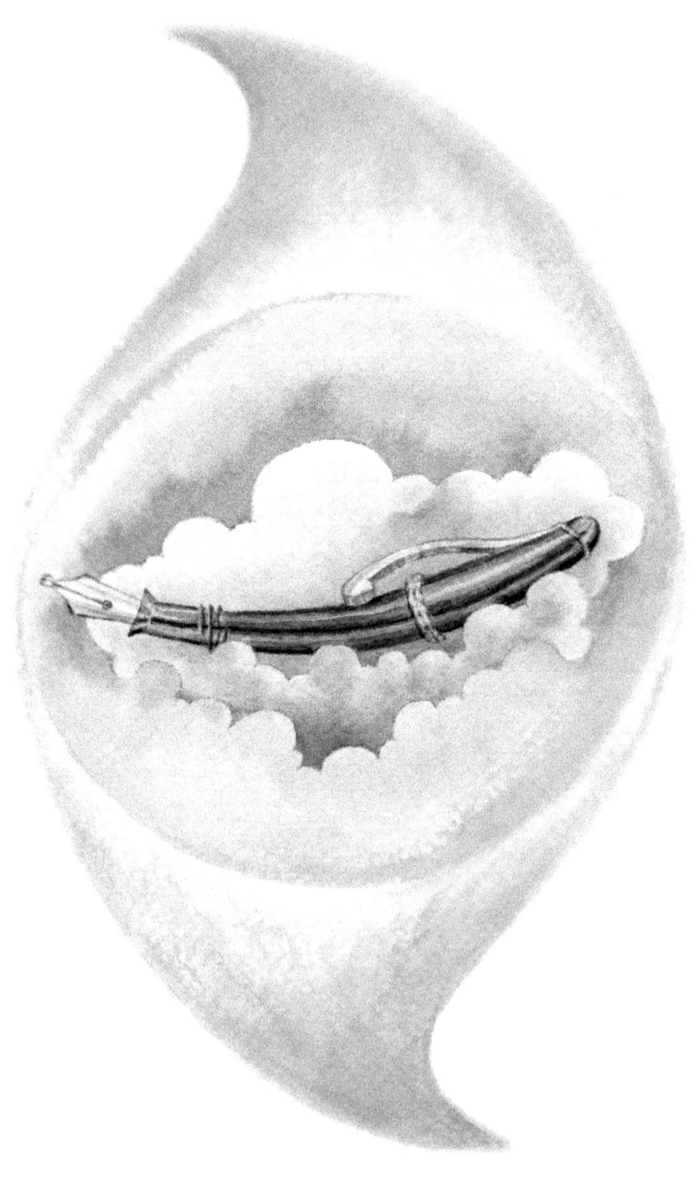

the worries
writ large
on the face
of that
destitute child
while the traffic signal
still paused !

If only
I could
shoot to end
the indictable lies
of those
despicable politicians
marauding
the
collective consciousness !

If only
I could
bring upon
through a magic wand –
a balming tsunami
on
the tormented millions !

If only
I could
relive
my lost childhood ,
under the

hawk - eyed
ever - protective
parental shadows !

If only
there was
a life
beyond life ;
to still try
to zoom upon
the meaning
of that
four - letter word
called
Wish !

MEMORIES

Memories
are those
which remain
during a lifetime
even though
the prized pictures
taken
through
the high - end handset
corrupt !

Memories are
like souls
those do not
die down
and remain
with your loved ones !

Memories are
those life events –
some we
try hard
to build
while some
just get
latched onto !

Memories are
the frames

those get
scanned
by the mind –
privately and secured !

In the
journey of life,
memories are
your constant companion,
with a choice
of what
one
wishes to retrieve
and
keep moving on !!!